My Holiday in

Greece

Susie Brooks

First published in 2008 by Wayland

First published in paperback in 2011

Copyright © Wayland 2008

Wayland
338 Euston Road
London NW1 3BH

Wayland Australia
Level 17/207 Kent Street
Sydney NSW 2000

Senior Editor: Claire Shanahan
Designer: Elaine Wilkinson
Map artwork: David le Jars

Brooks, Susie
My holiday in Greece
1. Vacations - Greece - Juvenile literature 2. Recreation -
Greece - Juvenile literature 3. Greece - Juvenile
literature 4. Greece - Social life and customs -
21st century - Juvenile literature
I. Title II. Greece
914.9'5'0476

ISBN 978 0 7502 6697 0

Cover: Tourists on the Acropolis in Athens © Daniella Nowitz/Corbis; Greek food Dave © Bartruff/Corbis.

p5: © Joyce Bentley; p6: © Geoff du Feu/Alamy; p7: © Jennie Hart/Alamy; p8, title page: © Todd A.
Gipstein/Corbis; p9: © Barry Lewis/Corbis; p10: © Walter Bibikow/JAI/Corbis; p11: © Silwen Randebrock/Alamy;
p12: © Daniella Nowitz/Corbis; p13: © Jon Hicks/Corbis; p14: © Werner Otto/Alamy; p15: © imagebroker/Alamy;
p16: © Danita Delimont/Alamy; p17: © FAN travelstock/Alamy; p18: © Peter M. Wilson/Alamy; p19: © Rod
Edwards/Alamy; p20: © Dave Bartruff/Corbis; p21: © Dorling Kindersley; p22: © Edward Parker/Alamy;
p23: © Kuttig - Travel/Alamy; p24: © James Davis Photography/Alamy; p25: © Owen Franken/Corbis; p26:
© Jack Carey/Alamy; p27: © IML Image Group Ltd/Alamy; p28: © Roger Cracknell 01/classic/Alamy; p29:
© IML Image Group Ltd/Alamy; Rita Storey/Wishlist; p31: © Greek School.

Printed in China

Wayland is a division of Hachette Children's Books, an Hachette UK company.

www.hachette.co.uk

Contents

This is Greece! 4

Summer hotspot 6

Cool houses 8

All aboard! 10

Exciting Athens 12

A trip back in time 14

Island worlds 16

On the rocks 18

Greek feasts 20

Time to shop 22

Local life 24

Great games 26

Fun celebrations 28

Play it yourself 30

Useful words 32

This is Greece!

Greece is a hilly country in south-east Europe. It sticks out into the sea and includes many islands. The easiest way to get here is by aeroplane.

Greece has lots of places to visit – this book will show you a few.

BLUE CAVE SHIPWRECK
GLASS BOTTOM BOAT
FROM THE NEAREST POINT
EVERY 10MIN. A BOAT LEAVES
ΓΑΛΑΖΙΑ ΣΠΗΛΙΑ ΝΑΥΑΓΙΟ
ΤΟ ΚΟΝΤΙΝΟΤΕΡΟ ΣΗΜΕΙΟ
ΞΕΝΑΓΗΣΗ ΜΕΣΑ ΣΤΑ ΣΠΗΛΑΙΑ
ΚΑΘΕ 10ΛΕΠΤΑ ΑΝΑΧΩΡΕΙ ΣΚΑΦΟΣ
POTAMITIS BROTHERS
TO BLUE CAVES & SHIPI

Many people choose just one Greek island for their holiday. Others travel around. Wherever you go, you will notice things that are different from home.

The Greek language has its own alphabet – the bottom half of this sign is written in it.

We raced to be first to see the sea. I saw it from the plane window!

Speak Greek!

hi
giásou (yah-sou)
yes
né (neh)
no
óhi (**oh**-hee)

5

Summer hotspot

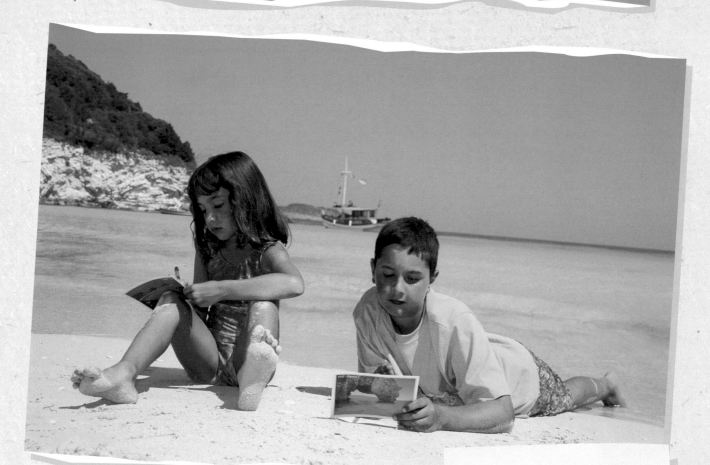

Greece is a popular place for summer holidays. The weather is hot and sunny and you are never too far from the sea.

Greece has lots of sandy beaches. This one is on the island of Antipaxos.

The middle of the day was hottest – we sat under an umbrella to keep out of the sun.

July and August can be sweltering and very busy! June and September are good times to visit. In winter, most of Greece is cool and rainy.

It's important to put on plenty of sun cream to stop your skin from burning.

Speak Greek!

beach
paralîa (pa-ra-**lee**-ya)
hot
zestó (zess-**t**oh)
cold
kryó (kree-yoh)

Cool houses

Near the Greek seaside there are many hotels, **villas** and **apartments** to stay in. They may have a swimming pool and terraces for sunbathing.

Some hotels have a pool on the roof!

I found a little lizard running up my bedroom wall! Dad said it was a gecko.

Houses are stacked high in the hillside village of Oia on Santorini island.

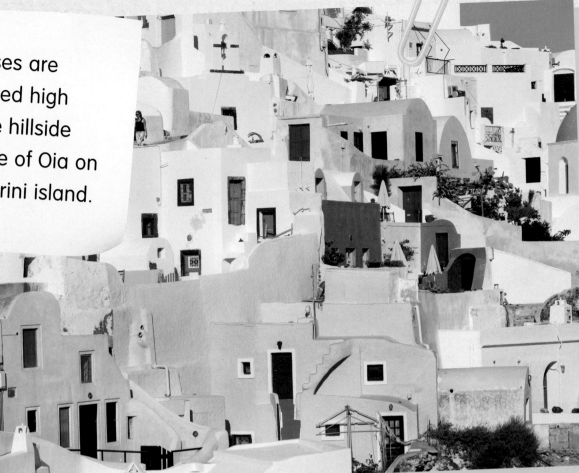

Many Greek villages are built on hillsides. The houses are made of stone and are often painted white to keep them cool inside.

Handy gadgets

• Mosquito plug or coil – to keep biting insects away!

• Plug adaptor – the plug sockets are different in Greece.

• Mini-fan – to keep you cool!

9

All aboard!

Huge ferries take people and cars to the larger islands.

You will probably go on a boat at some point during your holiday — especially if you visit an island.

Speak Greek!

bus
leoforío (lay-o-for-**ee**-yo)

taxi
taksí (tack-**see**)

passenger boat
plîo (plee-yoh)

10

Greek roads can be winding, and many towns and villages have narrow streets. Scooters and motorcycles are popular ways to get around.

The tiny island of Hydra has no cars. Instead people use donkeys or **mules**.

There were big waves when we went on the ferry – everything rocked and I felt seasick!

Exciting Athens

Athens is the capital of Greece. One sight everyone wants to see here is the Parthenon – an ancient temple on a hill called the Acropolis.

It's a long climb up the Acropolis, but worth it – wear good shoes!

People said the Parthenon changed colour in the evening light – and it really did!

You get a great view of the city from the Parthenon. Around the ancient parts of Athens, the streets are lively and modern.

You can watch the changing of the guard in Syntagma Square.

Things to do...

Run around in the National Gardens
Go back in time at the Children's Museum
Take a train up inside Lykavitos Hill

13

A trip back in time

Imagine living in ancient Greece, thousands of years ago! Wherever you go, look for clues like these...

Theatres

The **ancient Greeks** loved watching a show.

You can still sit on the seats at the Epidauros theatre.

Temples

People worshipped lots of gods in ancient **temples**. There is a famous one at Delphi.

This is the throne room of King Minos in the palace of Knossos, on the island of Crete.

Palaces

Grand palaces were built for ancient Greek kings. The walls have crumbled over the years, but you can still see treasures inside!

Island worlds

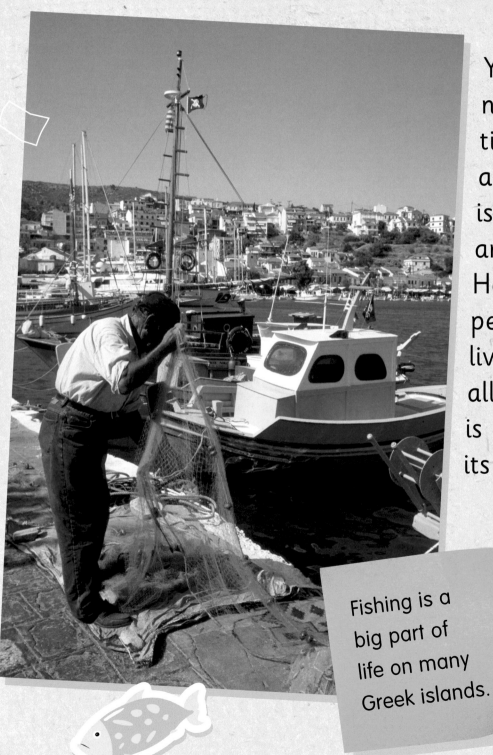

You would need a lot of time to explore all the Greek islands – there are thousands. However, people don't live on them all. Each island is special in its own way.

Fishing is a big part of life on many Greek islands.

16

Some people go on sailing holidays around groups of islands. With a boat, you can reach beaches that no one else can get to.

If you go to Mykonos, you might meet the local hero – Petros the pelican!

Island fun

Corfu – swim in clear blue sea

Kos – find beaches with white or black sand

Rhodes – see a real castle and build one on the beach

On the rocks

Away from the coast, much of Greece is made up of mountains. These are great places for walking, climbing, river rafting and watching wildlife.

Mountain goats are some of the best climbers in Greece!

I saw a snake – it didn't bite me, but it made me jump!

In the Meteora area in central Greece, **monasteries** mysteriously perch on tall towers of rock.

Monks still live up here – you can visit them, if you can work out how!

Shy animals to spot

- wolves
- brown bears
- lynx (wild cats)

Greek feasts

You'll find all your favourite food in Greece, but don't be afraid to try new things! Greek food is colourful and tasty.

Greeks eat a healthy diet of salad with olive oil, bread and lots of fish and seafood.

I got sticky eating souvlaki - you wrap up meat and salad in a yummy pocket of pitta bread.

For breakfast you might have Greek yoghurt with honey from local bees. Crispy cheese pies or pitta bread with dips make good snacks.

Most beaches have a **taverna** where you can eat outside.

On the menu

horiátiki (o-ree-a-tee-kee) - **Greek salad – with feta cheese, tomatoes, olives**

moussaka (moo-**sah**-ka) - **creamy aubergine and meat pie**

baklava (ba-**klah**-va) - **sticky honey and nut pastry**

Time to shop

Not all Greek villages have shops, so you might need to travel to find one. Many people buy their food in local markets.

Do you like olives? You'll find plenty of them grown and sold in Greece!

If you want to buy a **souvenir** to take home, look for handmade crafts or something that reminds you of your holiday. You'll need to change your money to euros.

Natural sponges from the bottom of the sea are cheap presents to buy for friends back home.

Presents to buy

Colourful rugs and cloths

Painted pots and plates

Olive oil made from olives

Local life

Nothing happens in a hurry in Greece, so get ready to relax! The Greek people love sitting and chatting, snoozing in the afternoon and staying up late.

You will often see Greek families sitting on their doorsteps in village streets.

This priest is preparing to baptise a child in a Greek Orthodox Church.

Most Greek people are members of the **Orthodox Church**. Children are named after saints and they celebrate their saint's day as well as their birthday.

Celebrate a name

Yannis (John) 7 January

Elisabet (Elisabeth, Lisa) 24 April

Thoma (Thomas, Tom) 6 October

Annis (Anna) 9 December

Great games

In 2004, thousands of people came to Athens to watch the **Olympic Games**. The first Olympics were held here more than 2,000 years ago!

You can still run on the track at the ancient Olympic site.

Sport is very popular in Greece, especially football. The seaside is great for volleyball as well as swimming, windsurfing and other watersports.

Parasailing is as good as flying! You land with a splash in the sea.

It was fun flying a kite with some Greek children on the beach.

Fun celebrations

If you come to Greece in February, look out for Apokries. This is the Greek carnival that happens before **Lent**. It's a time for parties and fancy dress parades.

During Apokries, the islanders of Skyros dance in traditional clothes.

Cracking red eggs is an Easter tradition. If yours stays whole, you'll get good luck!

Easter is one of the biggest festivals in Greece. People celebrate with church ceremonies, candle lighting, family feasts and games.

Make a date

1 January look for a coin in your Vasilopitta cake - you'll be lucky all year!	25 March watch soldiers march in big Independence Day parades.		

Play it yourself

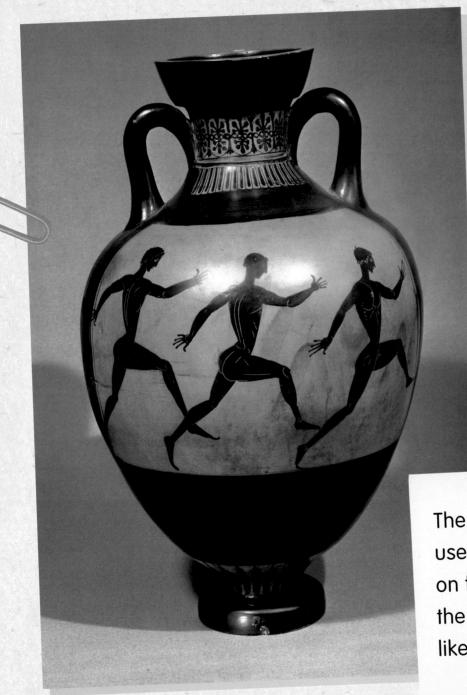

Pretend to be an athlete in the first Olympic Games! In ancient times, only men were allowed to compete, but girls can play this too!

The ancient Greeks used to run races on foot as part of the Olympics, just like we do now.

Event 1: Discus

Mark a spot to stand on. Throw the frisbee as far as you can. Measure the distance from the standing spot to the frisbee. Take turns and see whose throw is longest.

You will need:
- a large outdoor space
- sticks or markers
- a frisbee
- a long measuring tape.

Event 2: Chariot race

Mark a start and finish point. Line up in pairs and have a wheelbarrow race. The person on their hands is the horse – neigh all the way!

Event 3: Long jump

Mark a take-off point. Run up to it and then jump as far as you can. Measure the distance and see who jumps furthest.

Prizes

Crown your winners with **wreaths** made of real or paper leaves stuck to a hair band.

TIP: Invent other fun events. Ancient Greeks ran with shields and helmets – you could make your own!

Useful words

ancient Greeks   The people who lived in Greece and other parts of Europe thousands of years ago.

apartment   A room or flat for living in.

Lent   The 40 days leading up to Easter when Christians traditionally give something up.

monastery   A place where monks live a religious lifestyle.

mule   A cross between a donkey and a horse.

Olympic Games   The worldwide sports contest that happens every four years and first began in ancient Greece.

Orthodox Church   The main religious group in Greece and many other eastern European countries.

souvenir   Something you take home to remind you of somewhere you have been.

taverna   A Greek restaurant.

temple   A building for worshipping gods in.

villa   A home in the countryside.

wreath   A ring of leaves or flowers. Ancient Greeks wore wreaths made from olive branches.